APPLIED ART

in FINLAND

LES ARTS APPLIQUES EN FINLANDE
LAS ARTES UTILES EN FINLANDIA

THIS PUBLICATION presents illustrations of Applied Art in Finland, most of them reproducing objects designed and made during the last ten years.

Of all the creations of Handicraft and Industrial Art in Finland in recent years, those of textile must undoubtedly be placed in the front rank. The most characteristic of them is the hand-knotted "ryijy". Its technique has a long ancestry in the art of the peasantry. The rich colourings and imaginative designs have, to a high degree, inspired the art of modern textiles.

Furniture Designing and Interior Decoration in Finland originated in the old "estate culture" of the country. The modern style began to dawn at the turn of the century with the search for a Finnish national style, but this was soon followed by a neo-classic trend. The social revolution and dwelling reforms of the post-war period finally gave rise to the simplicity and practicableness which to-day characterise the art of interior decoration in the country.

Remarkable achievement can be recorded within the Glass and Pottery branches. Here it is chiefly the leading manufacturers who, in co-operation with skilled artists, have done so much. But independent artists have also actively contributed to the development observable.

Special interest has been devoted to the solution of illumination problems. Both technically and artistically the lighting fittings are on a very high level.

Graphic Art is in process of rapid development, and there are many fine workers in the other branches of Industrial Art.

Most of those engaged in Applied Art have been trained at the Central School of Industrial Art in Helsinki, which is maintained with public funds by the Society for Industrial Art in Finland. By annual exhibitions and other means of propaganda, this society has done much to raise the general taste of the country.

Working with this Society is the Applied Art Association in Finland — "Ornamo" — whose membership includes most of the artists engaged in this work. It was originally an unpretentious group of working artists, but it has gradually become a real professional union, and has won respect as an authority on all questions affecting Handicrafts and Industrial Art.

CETTE PUBLICATION renferme un certain nombre de reproductions des arts appliqués de la Finlande. Les illustrations représentent surtout des objets exécutés au cours des dix dernières années.

Dans l'ensemble de la production finlandaise pendant ces dernières décennies pour les industries d'art et pour les travaux manuels, la branche textile peut sans contredit être mise au premier plan. Les tissus les plus caractéristiques pour le pays sont les tapis appelés "ryijyt" et noués à la main. Cette technique de tissage a une longue tradition dans l'art populaire. Les couleurs bariolées et les dessins fantaisistes des vieux tapis ont inspiré à un haut degré l'art textile moderne.

L'art du meuble et de l'aménagement en Finlande tire son origine de la tradition des vieux manoirs du pays. A la fin du XIXe siècle, on assiste à l'irruption d'un style moderne visant à un caractère national finnois nettement marqué, et que suivit cependant bientôt une tendance néo-classique. Les changements sociaux de l'après-guerre et la réforme des logements firent finalement apparaître la simplicité et la solidité qui caractérisent l'art finlandais de l'ameublement d'aujourd'hui.

Dans la verrerie et la céramique, on a atteint ces dernières années des résultats remarquables. Ce sont surtout les grandes fabriques qui, avec la collaboration d'artistes de valeur, ont fourni le principal apport, mais l'action des artistes indépendants a aussi contribué efficacement au développement de ces arts.

La solution du problème de l'éclairage a été étudiée avec un intérêt particulier. L'armature des lampes est parvenue à un niveau remarquable, tant au point de vue technique qu'au point de vue artistique.

Les arts graphiques sont en plein essor et les autres branches des arts industriels disposent de praticiens de mérite.

La plupart des artistes décorateurs ont reçu leur formation à l'École Centrale des Arts décoratifs à Helsinki, qui est entretenue par la Société des Arts décoratifs de Finlande avec l'aide financière de l'État. Grâce à des expositions annuelles et à d'autres moyens de propagande, cette Société a beaucoup contribué à développer le goût en Finlande.

A côté de celle-ci, la Société Ornamo des arts industriels de Finlande, qui groupe la plupart des praticiens des arts appliqués et qui n'était à l'origine qu'une modeste réunion de camarades, est devenue avec les années une véritable association professionnelle qui a su s'imposer au dehors comme une autorité dans toutes les questions touchant les arts appliqués et industriels.

En LA PRESENTE PUBLICACIÓN salen un número de ilustraciones de arte útil finlandés. Las ilustraciones reproducen principalmente objetos que han visto la luz durante los últimos diez años.

De todas las industrias artísticas y trabajos de mano creados en Finlandia durante esta última decena deben sin exageración figurar en primer lugar los trabajos textiles. Los tejidos más característicos del país son los tapices de nudo hechos a mano, los llamados ryijyt. La técnica de estos tejidos procede del antiguo arte rural. El vivo colorido y la rica fantasía de los dibujos de estos antiguos tapices han servido también en alto grado para inspirar los trabajos del moderno arte textil.

El arte del mueble y la decoración interior en Finlandia tiene su origen de inspiración en la tradición de las antiguas casas señoriales del país. Entre final y comienzo del siglo apareció el estilo moderno que aspiró a introducirse en el estilo nacional finlandés, pero pronto fué reemplazado por una nueva tendencia hacia lo neoclásico. Las transformaciones sociales posteriores a la guerra mundial, y la reforma de las viviendas, dieron finalmente origen a la sencillez práctica que caracteriza la decoración interior finlandesa de hoy.

En el ramo del cristal y la cerámica, durante los últimos años, se han obtenido notables resultados debidos en gran parte a las principales fábricas de estas industrias en cooperación con artistas eminentes. Pero también la actividad de artistas independientes ha contribuído eficazmente al desarrollo de estas industrias.

La solución del problema del alumbrado ha sido atendido con especial interés. Las armaduras para el alumbrado han alcanzado tanto técnica como artísticamente una gran perfección.

En el arte gráfico se está obteniendo un rápido desarrollo, y en las demás artes industriales encontramos personal de gran mérito.

Casi todos los artistas que trabajan en las artes útiles han recibido su instrucción en la Escuela Central de Artes Útiles de Helsinki, mantenida con la ayuda financiera del Estado por la Asociación de Artes Útiles de Finlandia. Por medio de exposiciones anuales y otras informaciones activas esta Asociación ha contribuído en alto grado a hacer amar el arte en el país.

Junto a la mencionada Asociación trabaja la Confederación de industrias artísticas de Finlandia, llamada "Ornamo", que reune casi todos los trabajadores de las artes útiles. Esta Sociedad que primitivamente fué una reunión modesta de compañeros, se ha transformado con el transcurso de los años en un verdadero Sindicato profesional que ha logrado hacerse respetar por todos como autoridad en cuantas cuestiones se relacionan a oficios e industrias artísticas.

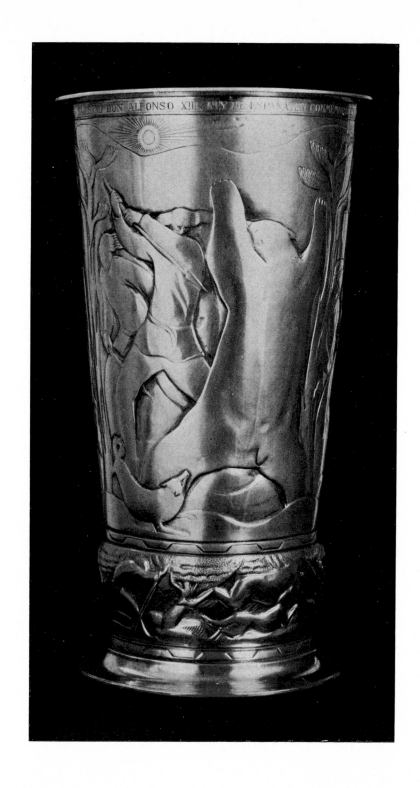

HENRY ERICSSON: Cup in chased silver - Coupe en argent ciselé - Copa
de plata cincelada (1929)   O.Y. Taito A.B.

MAIJA KANSANEN: Tapestry - Tapisserie - Tapiz

MAIJA KANSANEN: Decorative wall-hanging - Tapisserie décorative - Alfombrilla decorativa

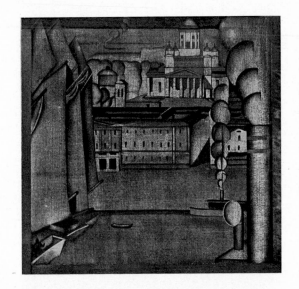

HENRY ERICSSON: Inlaid panels on the doors of the
cabinet on the opposite page. Motifs from Helsinki
- Panneaux en marqueterie de l'armoire ci-contre.
Motifs de Helsinki - Incrustaciones para los tableros del
armario de la página opuesta. Motivos de Helsinki

W. WEST: Cabinet in the office of the Mayor of Helsinki. Executed in birch by A.B. Stockmann O.Y. (Kerava Cabinet Works, Ltd.). Inlaid panels designed by Henry Ericsson (1929) - Armoire-archives en bouleau au bureau du Maire de Helsinki. A.B. Stockmann O.Y. (Menuiserie de Kerava S.A.). Panneaux en marqueterie par Henry Ericsson (1929) - Armario-archivador de abedul, en la oficina del alcalde de Helsinki. A.B. Stockmann O.Y. (Ebanistería de Kerava S.A.). El dibujo de la incrustación de los tableros, diseñado por Henry Ericsson (1929)

GUNNAR FORSSTRÖM: Inlaid panel in the Smoking-room of S/S Bore II. Executed by O.Y. Boman A.B., Turku - Panneau en marqueterie du fumoir du paquebot Bore II, exécuté par O.Y. Boman A.B., Turku - Tablero con incrustaciones en el salón de fumar del vapor "Bore II". Ejecutados por O.Y. Boman A.B. Turku

Engraved glass, designed by
the gifted artist HENRY
ERICSSON, who died in
1933. Riihimäki Glassworks

Verreries gravées, dessinées
par l'éminent artiste HENRY
ERICSSON, mort en 1933.
Verrerie de Riihimäki

6

Grabados en cristal, dibujados por el eminente artista
HENRY ERICSSON muerto
en 1933. Fábrica de cristal
de Riihimäki

7

ELSA ELENIUS: Pottery - Urne - Alfa-
rería

ELSA ELENIUS: Pottery - Céramiques
- Cerámicas

KURT EKHOLM: Vases in stoneware, executed by O.Y. Arabia A.B. - Vases de grès. exécutés par O.Y. Arabia A.B. - Jarrones de barro, ejecutados por O.Y. Arabia A.B.

ELSA ELENIUS: Pottery - Céramiques - Cerámicas

Textile-designer at her drawing-board - Dessinatrice de textiles à sa table de travail - Delineante de tejidos en su mesa de trabajo

VIOLA GRÅSTEN: Rug (Ryijy) - Tapis - Alfombra decorativa
Suomen Käsityön Ystävät

Hand-loom weaving - Tissage au métier - Tejiendo en telar de mano

10

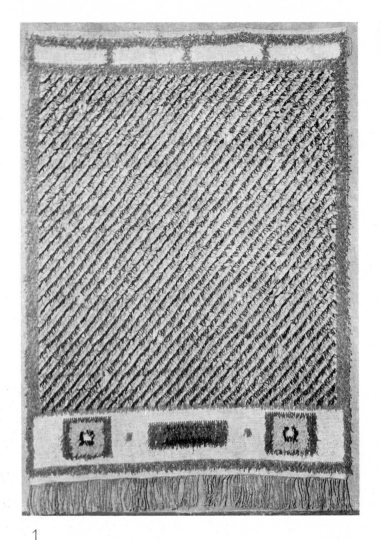
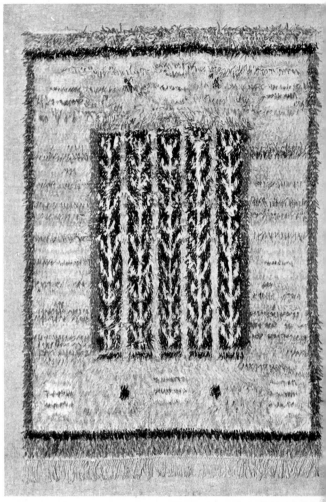

1   2

1   EVA EKLÖF: Rug (Ryijy) - Tapis   - Alfombra decorativa
                           Suomen Käsityön Ystävät
2   GUNILLA JUNG: Rug (Ryijy) - Tapis - Alfombra decorativa
                           Suomen Käsityön Ystävät

Left, VIOLA GRÅSTEN: Rug (Ryijy). Right, TOINI NYSTRÖM: Rug. Both executed by Suomen Käsityön Ystävät

A gauche: VIOLA GRÅSTEN: Tapis (Ryijy). A droite: TOINI NYSTRÖM: Tapis. Exécutés l'un et l'autre par Suomen Käsityön Ystävät

A la izquierda: VIOLA GRÅSTEN: Alfombra decorativa (Ryijy). A la derecha: TOINI NYSTRÖM: Alfombra decorativa Ejecutadas por la Suomen Käsityön Ystävät

IMPI SOTAVALTA: Rug (Ryijy) - Tapis - Alfombra decorativa   Suomen Käsityön Ystävät

Left, GRETE HERMANSEN: Rug (Ryijy). Right, EVA BRUMMER: Rug. Both executed by Suomen Käsityön Ystävät

A gauche, GRETE HERMANSEN: Tapis (Ryijy). A droite, EVA BRUMMER: Tapis. Exécutés l'un et l'autre par Suomen Käsityön Ystävät

A la izquierda, GRETE HERMANSEN: Alfombra decorativa (Ryijy). A la derecha, EVA BRUMMER: Alfombra decorativa Ejecutadas por Suomen Käsityön Ystävät

13

14

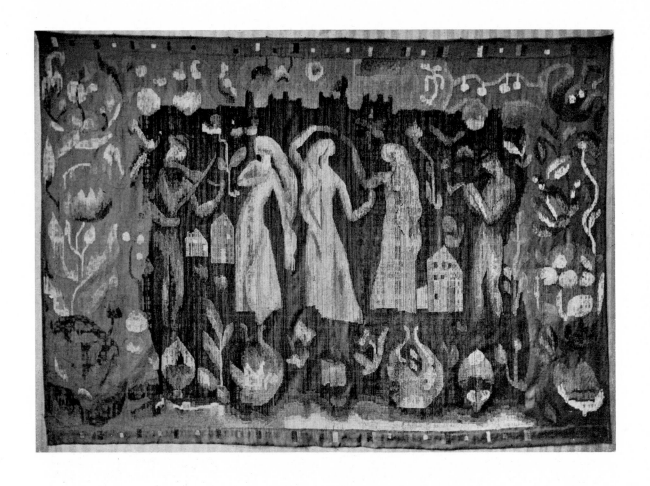

EVA ANTTILA: Two tapestries. Left, "The Middle Ages in Finland". Right, "The Spring". Executed by the artist

Deux tapisseries. A gauche, "Le moyen âge en Finlande". A droite: "Le printemps". Exécutées par l'artiste

Dos tapices: A la izquierda, "La Edad media en Finlandia". A la derecha: "La Primavera". Ejecutados por el artista

MARGARETA AHLSTEDT-WILLANDT: Tapestry.
Executed by the artist - Tapisserie exécutée par
l'artiste - Tapiz. Ejecutado por el artista

16

SIGRID WIKSTRÖM: Tapestry, executed in 1911
- Tapisserie exécutée en 1911 - Tapiz. Ejecutado
en 1911

17

ALLI KOROMA: Fabric in a typical Finnish technique, executed at the Central School of Applied Art, Helsinki - Tissu typique, à la finlandaise, exécuté par l'École Centrale des Arts Appliqués, Helsinki - Tejido, manufacturación característica de Finlandia. Ejecutado por la Escuela Central de Artes Ùtiles. Helsinki
Photo Kolmio

LISA JOHANSSON: Rug (Ryijy) - Tapis - Alfombra decorativa
Suomen Käsityön Ystävät

KREETA POHJANHEIMO: Linen rug, executed
by the artist - Tapis de lin, exécuté par l'artiste
- Tapiz de lino, ejecutado por el artista
Photo Pietinen

LEA VEHMANEN: Fabric in a typical Finnish
technique, executed at the Central School of
Applied Art, Helsinki - Tissu typique à la fin-
landaise, exécuté par l'École Centrale des Arts
Appliqués, Helsinki - Tejido, manufacturación
característica de Finlandia. Ejecutado por la
Escuela Central de Artes Ùtiles, Helsinki
Photo Kolmio

KIRSTI SYVÄRANTA: Fabric in the same technique, executed at the Central School of Applied Art, Helsinki - Tissu à la finlandaise.
Exécuté par l'École Centrale des Arts appliqués,
Helsinki - Tejido de la misma técnica ejecutado
por la Escuela Central de Artes Ùtiles, Helsinki
Photo Kolmio

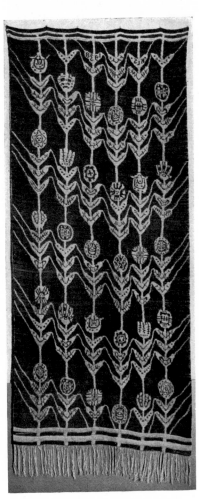

19

MARIANNE STRENGELL: Plaid - Plaid -
Manta con diseño
A.B Hemflit - Kotiahkeruus O.Y

[KREETA POHJANHEIMO: Woollen Scarf -
Cravate de laine - Bufanda de lana

GRETA SKOGSTER-LEHTINEN:
Furnishing-fabrics - Tissus d'intérieur - Manufacturas útiles

MARGA TIKKANEN: Fa-
brics - Tissus - Tejidos
Photo Kolmio

GRETA SKOGSTER-LEHTINEN: Fabric - Tissu - Tejido
Photo Rasmussen

GRETA SITTNIKOW: Fabrics - Tissus - Tejidos
Photo Kolmio

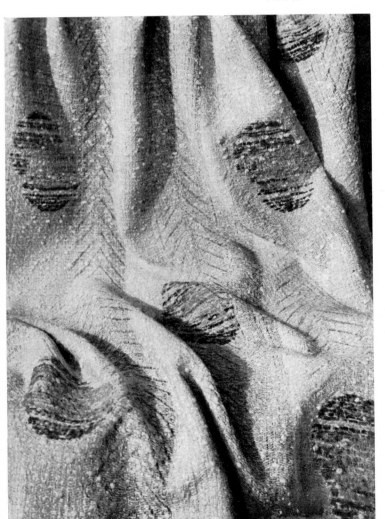

EVA ANTTILA: Tapestry, executed by the artist - Tapisserie, exécutée par l'artiste - Tapiz, ejecutado por el artista

EVA ANTTILA: Tapestry "Midsummer Fires" ("Juhannus Kokko"), executed by the artist - Tapisserie "Le feu de la Saint-Jean" exécutée par l'artiste - Tapiz "Las hogueras de San Juan" ("Juhannus Kokko") ejecutado por el artista

22

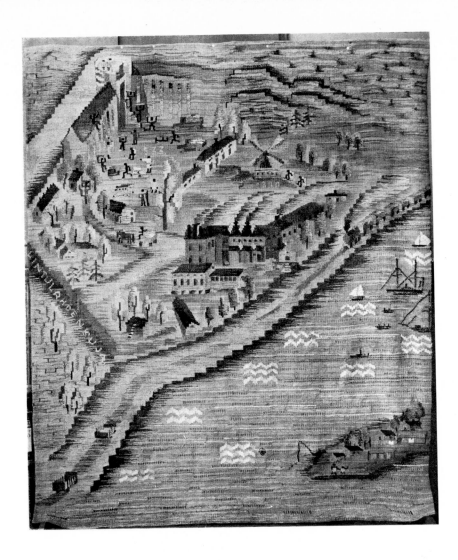

GRETA SKOGSTER-LEHTINEN:
Tapestry - Tapisserie - Tapiz

EVA ANTTILA: Tapestry "Helsinki", executed by the Artist - Tapisserie "Helsinki", exécutée par l'artiste - Tapiz "Helsinki", ejecutado por el artista

W. WEST: Armchair in walnut, covered in handwoven woollen fabric and executed by A.B. Stockmann O.Y. (Kerava Cabinet Works, Ltd.) - Fauteuil en noyer couvert d'une étoffe blanche en laine et exécuté par A.B. Stockmann O.Y. (Menuiserie de Kerava S.A.) - Sillón de nogal, cubierto de lana tejida a mano, ejecutado por A.B. Stockmann O.Y. (Ebanistería de Kerava Ltd) Photo Kolmio

MARGARET T. NORDMAN: Armchair and table in walnut, executed by A.B. Stockmann O.Y. (Kerava Cabinet Works, Ltd.) - Fauteuil et table en noyer, exécutés par A.B. Stockmann O.Y. (Menuiserie de Kerava S.A.) - Sillón y mesa de nogal, ejecutados por A.B. Stockmann O.Y. (Ebanistería de Kerava Ltd.) Photo Kolmio

W. WEST and MARGARET T. NORDMAN: Living-room, panelled in pine-wood with furniture in walnut, executed by A.B. Stockmann O.Y. (Kerava Cabinet Works, Ltd.). Rug and fabrics designed by Marga Tikkanen - Salon lambrissé en bois de pin avec mobilier en noyer. Exécutée par A.B. Stockmann O.Y. (Menuiserie de Kerava S.A.). Tapis et tissus dessinés par Marga Tikkanen - Habitación de estar, tableros de madera de pino, muebles de nogal, ejecutados por A.B. Stockmann O.Y. (Ebanistería de Kerava S.A.). Alfombra y tejidos dibujados por Marga Tikkanen

MARGARET T. NORDMANN: Furniture, executed by O.Y. Boman A.B., Turku - Mobilier, exécuté par O.Y. Boman A.B., Turku - Muebles ejecutados por O.Y. Boman A.B., Turku

GUNNEL NYMAN: Armchair and table in American walnut, executed by the Huhta Workshops, Hämeenlinna - Fauteuil et table en noyer américain, exécutés par la Menuiserie Huhta, Hämeenlinna - Sillón y mesa de nogal americano, ejecutados por la Carpintería Huhta, Hämeenlinna

W. WEST: Living-room with dining-table in front of the window. Furniture executed by A.B. Stockmann O.Y. (Kerava Cabinet Works Ltd.). Plywood chairs by Wilh. Schaumans Fanérfabrik A.B. - Salon avec table à manger devant la fenêtre. Mobilier exécuté par A.B. Stockmann O.Y. (Menuiserie de Kerava S.A.). Chaises en bois contreplaqué de O.Y. Wilh. Schaumans Fanérfabrik AB. - Habitación de estar con mesa de comer delante de la ventana. Muebles ejecutados por A.B. Stockmann O.Y. (Ebanistería de Kerava S.A.). Sillas con chapas de madera, por O.Y. Wilh. Schaumans Fanerfabrik A.B.

Photo Kolmio

A. BRUMMER: Furniture for a study. Desk with chair and book-case, executed in polished imbuija. Left, Armchair, small smokers' table and rest chair for the same room. Upholstery in black leather. Executed by O.Y. Boman A.B., Turku - Table à écrire, chaise et bibliothèque pour studio, en imbuija polie A gauche: Fauteuil, petite table de fumeur et chaise-longue pour la même chambre. Garniture en cuir noir. Travail de la Menuiserie O.Y. Boman A.B., Turku - Mesa de escribir, silla y biblioteca, para habitación de estudio. Hecho en imbuija pulida. A la izquierda, sillón, mesita de fumar y hamaca para dicha habitación. Las sillas tapizadas de cuero negro. Ejecutado por O.Y. Boman A.B. Turku   Photo Kolmio

27

ALVAR AALTO: Paimio Sanatorium : Reading-room (1933) - Sanatorium de Paimio: Salle de lecture (1933) - Sanatorio de Paimio: Sala de lectura (1933)

AINO and ALVAR AALTO: Easy chairs with resilient birch plywood seats and backs (Paimio Sanatorium). Artek-model - Fauteuils à sièges et dossiers flexibles en bouleau contreplaqué (Sanatorium de Paimio). Modèle Artek - Butacones de asiento y respaldo flexibles, de contrachapeado de abedul (Paimio, Sanatorio). Modelo Artek

28

AINO and ALVAR AALTO: Easy chair and wall-bracket, Artek-model Birch - Fauteuil et étagère, modèle Artek. Bouleau - Sillón y estante de abedul, modelo Artek

AINO and ALVAR AALTO: Resilient easy chair, Artek-model. Birch - Fauteuil en porte-à-faux, modèle Artek. Bouleau - Sillón movible en abedul. Modelo Artek

ALVAR AALTO: From the Finnish Pavilion in Paris 1937; Section for Architecture with Artek furniture - Au pavillon finlandais de Paris 1937. Section d'Architecture. Mobilier modèle Artek - Del Pabellón finlandés de Paris 1937. Sección de Arquitectura con mobiliario modelos Artek

ILMARI TAPIOVAARA: Hotel bedroom.
Furniture in lacquered and natural birch,
executed by Asko, Lahti - Chambre d'hô-
tel. Meubles en bouleau naturel et teint,
exécutés par Asko, Lahti - Dormitorio
de Hotel. Muebles de abedul al natural y
barnizado. Ejecutado por Asko, Lahti

Photo Kolmio

ILMARI TAPIOVAARA: Corner of a room
at an Exhibition - Coin de chambre à une
Exposition - Rincón de una habitación
en una Exposición   Photo Kolmio

MAIJA HEIKINHEIMO: Cabinet - Chiffon-
nier - Armario-archivador
Liljamaa, Wiipuri. Railo, Helsinki
Photo Kolmio

GUNNEL NYMAN: Furniture from an Exhibition - Meubles d'une Exposition - Muebles de una exposición   Photo Kolmio

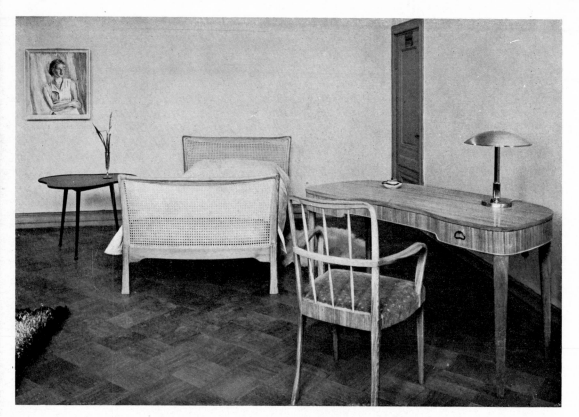

RUNAR ENGBLOM:
Bedroom furniture from
the Exhibition of Indu-
strial Art 1937, executed
by the Syhrén Work-
shops - Mobilier pour
chambre à coucher de
l'Exposition d'Arts Ap-
pliqués de 1937, exécuté
par la Menuiserie Syh-
rén - Muebles de dor-
mitorio de la Exposición
de Arte Industrial 1937,
ejecutados por la Car-
pinteria Syhrén

RUNAR ENGBLOM: Furnit-
ure for a living room, exhibited by Huonekalukeskus
at the Furniture Fair in Helsinki 1937 - Mobilier pour
salon, exposé par Huone-
kalukeskus à la Foire du
Mobilier de Helsinki 1937 -
Muebles para salita de estar,
expuestos por la Huonekalukeskus en la Exposición de
muebles de Helsinki 1937

RUNAR ENGBLOM: Furniture for a living room, exhibited by Huonekalukeskus at the Furniture Fair in Helsinki 1937 - Meubles de salon exposé par Huonekalukeskus à la Foire du Mobilier de Helsinki 1937 - Muebles de salita de estar, expuestos por la Huonekalukeskus en la Exposición de muebles de Helsinki 1937

RUNAR ENGBLOM: Chair - Chaise - Silla
Huonekalukeskus
Photo Kolmio

33

Drawing-room in a Helsinki flat, arranged by Artek, furniture by AINO and ALVAR AALTO (1936) - Salon d'un appartement à Helsinki, intérieur composé par Artek, meubles par AINO et ALVAR AALTO (1936) - Salón de una vivienda de Helsinki arreglado por Artek, muebles de AINO y ALVAR AALTO (1936)

W. WEST: Chairs, executed by Wilh. Schaumans Fanérfabrik A.B., Jyväskylä - Chaises, exécutées par Wilh. Schaumans Fanérfabrik A.B., Jyväskylä - Sillas, ejecutadas por Wilh. Schaumans Fanérfabrik A.B., Jyväskylä

Photo Roos

ILMARI TAPIOVAARA: Chair - Chaise - Silla
Photo Kolmio   Asko O.Y., Lahti

MARGARET T. NORDMAN: Nest of Tables
- Jeu de tables - Juego de mesitas
Photo Kolmio   A.B. Stockmann O.Y.

Private room of a Helsinki Restaurant, arranged by Artek, furniture by AINO and ALVAR AALTO
(1938) - Salon particulier dans un Restaurant de Helsinki, intérieur composé par Artek, meubles par
AINO et ALVAR AALTO (1938) - Salón privado en un Restaurant de Helsinki, arreglado por Artek,
muebles de AINO y ALVAR AALTO (1938)

ELNA KILJANDER: Study. Furniture in elm, executed by Koti-Hemmet - Studio. Mobilier en orme, exécuté par Koti-Hemmet - Cuarto de estudio. Muebles de olmo, ejecutados por Koti-Hemmet

Photo Pietinen

RUNAR ENGBLOM: Tea wagon - Table à thé roulante - Coche de té   O.Y. Viri A.B.

LISA JOHANSSON: Dining-room cabinet in mahogany - Armoire de salle à manger, en acajou - Armario de comedor, de caoba
A.B. Stockmann O.Y.

Photo Kolmio

GUNNEL NYMAN: Table
and chairs in polished imbuija - Table et chaises en
imbuija poli - Mesa y sillas
de imbuija pulida
O.Y. Boman A.B., Turku
Photo Rasmussen

MARGARET T. NORD-
MAN: Armchair and table
- Fauteuil et table - Sillón y
mesa A.B. Stockmann O.Y.
Photo Roos

37

GUNNEL NYMAN: Writing Cabinet - Secrétaire - Secreter   O.Y. Boman A.B.

EINARI KYÖSTILÄ: Living room. Furniture in elm, executed by A.B. Stockmann O.Y. (Kerava Cabinet Works Ltd.) - Salon. Mobilier en orme, exécuté par A.B. Stockmann O.Y. (Menuiserie de Kerava S.A.) - Habitación de estar. Muebles de olmo, ejecutados por A.B. Stockmann O.Y. (Ebanistería de Kerava, S.A.)

Photo Kolmio

W. WEST: Living room with dining recess from an Exhibition of standard models. Furniture in pine and birch, executed by the Finnish General Handicraft Association - Salon-salle à manger, d'une Exposition de modèles normalisés. Mobilier en pin et en bouleau, exécuté par l'Association Générale d'Arts Industriels de Finlande - Habitación de estar con comedor de esquina de una Exposición de modelos en serie. Muebles de pino y abedul ejecutados por la Asociación General de Oficios Manuales de Finlandia   Photo Kolmio

W. WEST: Chairs from the interior shown above - Chaises de l'intérieur ci-dessus - Sillas para el interior de arriba   Photo Kolmio

Government Council Room in the Parliament House. Architect: Professor J. S. Sirén. The ceiling in black, gold and grey. Blue carpet. Furniture designed by A. Brummer and executed in birch, palisander and walnut with gilded metal - Salle de séances du Gouvernement à la Chambre des Députés. Architecte: J. S. Sirén. Plafond en noir, en or et en gris. Tapis bleu. Meubles dessinés par A. Brummer. Matériaux: bouleau, palissandre et noyer garnis de métal doré - Sala de la Junta de Gobierno en la Cámara de Diputados. Arquitecto: Profesor . S. Sirén. Techo en negro, oro y gris. Alfombra azul. Muebles dibujados por A. Brummer y ejecutados en abedul, palisandro y nogal con adornos de metal dorado

A. BRUMMER: Presiding Member's chair in the Government Council Room. Executed in birch with gilded metal. Covered in black leather with embossed and gilded coat of arms - Chaise du président dans la salle de séances du Gouvernement à la Chambre des Députés, en bouleau garni de métal doré, tapissée en cuir noir avec armoiries dorées - Silla Presidencial en la Sala de la Junta de Gobierno en la Cámara de Diputados. Ejecutada en abedul con adornos de metal dorado y tapizado de cuero negro con escudo de armas en dorado

A. BRUMMER: Armchair and table in the Parliament House. The armchair in birch with gilded metal. The table in zebrano and metal - Fauteuil et table dans la Chambre des Députés. Le fauteuil en bouleau garni de métal doré. La table en zébrano et en métal - Sillón y mesa en la Cámara de Diputados. El sillón de abedul con adornos de metal dorado. La mesa de zebrano y metal

A. BRUMMER: Writing-desk in the Parliament House. Executed in zebrano and metal - Pupitre de la Chambre des Députés, en zébrano et en métal - Mesa escritorio en la Cámara de Diputados. Ejecutada en zebrano y metal

GUNNAR FINNE: Mural relief in the Café of the Parliament House - Panneau en relief du Café de la Chambre des Députés - Relieve mural en el café de la Cámara de Diputados

J. S. SIRÉN: Cabinet in the Parliament House executed in figured walnut. Carving by Hannes Autere - Armoire de la Chambre des Députés. Racine de noyer. Sculptures sur bois par Hannes Autere - Armario-archivador en la Cámara de Diputados, ejecutado en nogal labrado. Esculturas de madera por Hannes Autere

42

HANNES AUTERE: Wood-carvings on the cabinet on opposite page: "The Smith", "The Tailor", "The Shoemaker" and "The Carpenter" - Sculptures sur bois de l'armoire ci-contre: "Le Forgeron", "Le Tailleur", "Le Cordonnier" et "Le Menuisier" - Esculturas de madera en el armario-archivador de enfrente: "El Herrero", "El Sastre", "El Zapatero", "El Carpintero"

1

HANNES AUTERE: Four decorative wood-carvings representing different stages of lumbering: 1. Marking trees; 2. Felling timber; 3. Transporting logs; 4. Timber-floating - Quatre sculptures sur bois représentant les diverses étapes de l'exploitation des bois: 1. Le marquage des arbres; 2. L'abattage; 3. Le Transport des troncs; 4. Le flottage des troncs - Cuatro esculturas decorativas en madera representando diferentes escenas de la explotación de bosques: 1. Marca de árboles; 2. Corte de troncos; 3. Transporte de troncos; 4. Almadías

2

3

HANNES AUTERE: Wood-carving: "Whom thou lovest thou chastisest" - Sculpture sur bois: "Qui aime bien châtie bien" - Esculturas en madera: "Quien bien quiere bien castiga"

Photo Kolmio

4

HANNES AUTERE: "The Fisherman", wood-carving - Le pêcheur", sculpture sur bois - "El Pescador". Escultura en madera

MARGARET T. NORDMAN: Two cabinets in pine, executed by A.B. Stockmann O.Y. (Kerava Cabinet Works Ltd.). Carving by Hannes Autere - Deux chiffonniers. A.B. Stockmann O.Y. (Menuiseries de Kerava, S.A.). Sculpture sur bois par Hannes Autere - Dos armarios-archivadores de pino, ejecutados por A.B. Stockmann O.Y. (Ebanistería de Kerava, S.A.). Esculturas en madera de Hannes Autere   Photo Sauren — Iffland

Corner of a sitting-room in a Club. Textiles designed by Greta Skogster-Lehtinen. Table by Alvar Aalto. Armchair by Stockmann's Drawing-office - Coin de salle dans un cercle. Textiles dessinés par Greta Skogster-Lehtinen. Table par Alvar Aalto. Fauteuil par le bureau de dessin de A.B. Stockmann O.Y. - Rincón de una sala en un Club. Tejidos dibujados por Greta Skogster-Lehtinen. Mesa por Alvar Aalto. Sillón por la Oficina de Dibujo de Stockmann O.Y.

Photo Iffland

W. WEST: Chair in elm and cane, executed by Kerava Cabinet Works, Ltd. - Chaise en orme et en rotin, exécutée par la Menuiserie de Kerava S.A. - Silla de olmo y rejilla, ejecutada por la Ebanistería de Kerava, S.A.

NORA HENSCHEL and KAJ FRANCK: Printed cotton and linen fabrics, executed by The United Woollen Factories, Hyvinkää - Cretonnes de coton et de lin imprimées par les Manufactures Réunies de laine de Hyvinkää - Cretonas de algodón y tejidos de lino, ejecutados por "La Unión de Fábricas de Algodón" en Hyvinkää

47

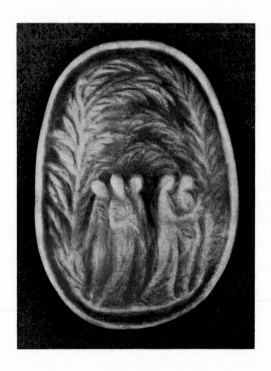 

EVA GYLDÉN: Cameos. Very subtle effect achieved by the colouring in the different
layers of the shell - Camées. Effet subtil obtenu par les diverses nuances des couches
du coquillage travaillé - Camafeos. Varios y primorosos efectos obtenidos por los diferentes colores de las capas de la concha trabajada

Photo Kolmio

W. WEST: Cabinet, decorated with lacquer-work, designed and executed by Henry Ericsson. A.B. Stockmann
O.Y. (Kerava Cabinet Works, Ltd.) (1926) - Chiffonnier
laqué, avec un décor de Henry Ericsson. A.B. Stockmann O.Y. (Menuiserie de Kerava S.A.) (1926) -
Armario-archivador con trabajos de laca dibujados y
ejecutados por Henry Ericsson. A.B. Stockmann O.Y.
(Ebanistería de Kerava, S.A.)

GUNNAR FINNE: Perfume-bottle, Riihimäki Glassworks - Flacon de parfum. Verreries de Riihimäki
- Frasco para perfume. Fábrica de cristal de Riihimäki

Glass-engraver at work - Graveur sur verre au travail
- Trabajos de cristal grabado

G. A. JYSKY: Crystal cup. Riihimäki Glassworks -
Coupe de cristal. Verrerie de Riihimäki - Copa de
cristal. Fábrica de cristal de Riihimäki   Photo Iffland

A. BRUMMER: Engraved glass bowl "Lapland", executed by Riihimäki Glassworks - Coupe en verre
gravé "Laponie", exécutée par la Verrerie de Riihimäki
- Copa de cristal grabado "Laponia" ejecutada por la
Fábrica de cristal de Riihimäki   Photo Pietinen

ARTTU BRUMMER: Engraved glass bowl.
Riihimäki Glassworks - Flacon en verre
gravé. Verrerie de Riihimäki - Copa
grabada de cristal, Fábrica de cristal de
Riihimäki   Photo Pietinen

GUNNEL NYMAN: Engraved glass bottle.
Riihimäki Glassworks - Flacon en verre
gravé. Verrerie de Riihimäki - Botella de
cristal grabado. Fábrica de cristal de Riihimäki   Photo Iffland

YRJÖ ROSOLA: Engraved glass bottle. Riihimäki Glassworks - Flacon en verre gravé.
Verrerie de Riihimäki - Botella de cristal
grabado. Fábrica de cristal de Riihimäki

Photo Iffland

ARTTU BRUMMER: Flower Vases. Riihimäki
Glassworks - Vases à fleurs. Verrerie de
Riihimäki - Floreros. Fábrica de cristal de
Riihimäki

Photo Kolmio

52

ARTTU BRUMMER: Flower Vases.
Riihimäki Glassworks - Vases à
fleurs. Verrerie de Riihimäki -
Floreros. Fábrica de cristal de Riihimäki   Photo Iffland

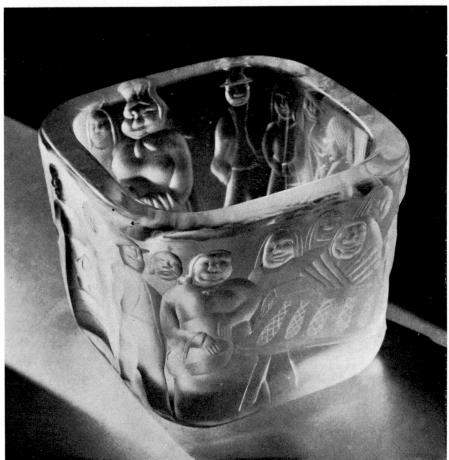

GUNNEL NYMAN: Engraved glass
bowl. Riihimäki Glassworks - Bol
en verre gravé. Verrerie de Riihimäki - Copa de cristal grabado.
Fábrica de Cristal de Riihimäki

GÖRAN HONGELL: Glass bowl. Karhula-Iittala Glassworks - Bol en verre. Verrerie de Karhula-Iittala - Copa de cristal. Fábrica de cristal de Karhula-Iittala
Photo Iffland

GUNNEL NYMAN: Engraved glass dish. Karhula-Iittala Glassworks - Bol en verre gravé. Verrerie Karhula-Iittala - Copa de cristal grabado. Fábrica de cristal Karhula-Iittala

Photo Iffland

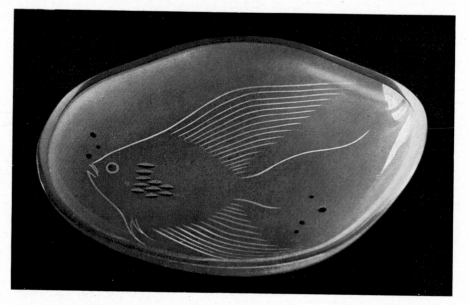

54

GÖRAN HONGELL: Glass bowl. Riihimäki Glassworks - Bol en verre. Verrerie de Riihimäki - Copa
de cristal. Fábrica de cristal de Riihimäki

Photo Iffland

WALTER WAHLROOS: Flower vase. Riihimäki Glassworks - Vase à fleurs. Verrerie de Riihimäki - Florero.
Fábrica de cristal de Riihimäki   Photo Kolmio

55

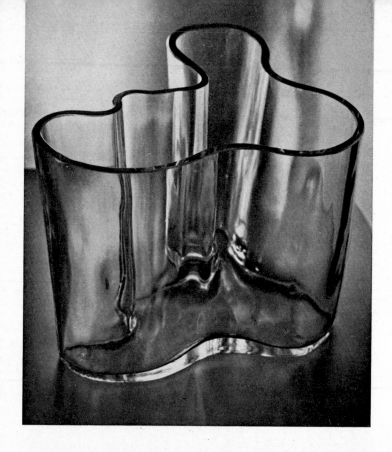

ALVAR AALTO: Flower bowl. Karhula-Iittala Glassworks - Coupe à fleurs. Verrerie de Karhula-Iittala - Jarrón para flores. Fábrica de cristal Karhula-Iittala

GÖRAN HONGELL: Crystal glass bowl. Karhula-Iittala Glassworks - Coupe en verre taillé. Verrerie de Karhula-Iittala - Copa de cristal tallado. Fábrica de cristal Karhula-Iittala

Photo Iffland

GUNNEL NYMAN: Glass
bowl. Riihimäki Glass-
works - Coupe de verre.
Verrerie de Riihimäki -
Copa de cristal. Fábrica
de cristal de Riihimäki

Photo Rasmussen

ARTTU BRUMMER: Flow-
er vase. Riihimäki Glass-
works - Vase à fleurs.
Verrerie de Riihimäki -
Florero. Fábrica de cristal
de Riihimäki   Photo Kolmio

AINO and ALVAR AALTO: Pressed glass, executed by Karhula-Iittala Glassworks - Verreterie moulée par la Verrerie de Karhula-Iittala - Cristal prensado, ejecutado por la Fábrica de cristal Karhula-Iittala

Photo Iffland

ARTTU BRUMMER: Chair - Chaise - Silla

W. WEST: Chair - Chaise - Silla

BARITA AMINOFF: Furnishing fabrics - Tissus d'intérieurs - Tejidos para interiores
A.B. Hemflit-Kotiahkeruus O.Y.

BRUNO ALM: Grocer's
shop, executed by Suo-
men Osuuskauppojen
Keskuskunta - Magasin
de denrées coloniales.
Aménagé par Suomen
Osuuskauppojen Kes-
kuskunta - Almacén de
ultramarinos, arreglado
por Suomen Osuuskaup-
pojen Keskuskunta

ft, W. WEST: Tobac-
nist's shop. A.B. Stock-
nn O.Y. (Kerava Ca-
et Works, Ltd.) -
gauche: W. WEST:
bit de tabac. A.B.
ockmann O.Y. (Menui-
rie de Kerava S.A.) -
la izquierda: W.
EST: Despacho de
bacos. A.B. Stockmann
Y. (Ebanistería de Ke-
va, S.A.)

WALTER WAHLROOS:
Window displays -
Devanture décorative -
Decorado de escaparate
A.B. Stockmann O.Y.
Photo Kolmio

61

Graphic Artist at work - Artiste graphique au travail - Trabajos gráficos para un cartel

P. SÖDERSTRÖM: Poster for the World Skiing Championship Competition, Lahti 1938 - Affiche pour les championnats du monde de ski à Lahti en 1938 - Cartel para el Campeonato Mundial de Skis, Lahti 1938

ILMARI SYSIMETSÄ: Poster for the Olympic Games in Helsinki 1940 - Affiche pour les Jeux Olympiques de Helsinki en 1940 - Cartel para los Juegos Olímpicos de Helsinki 1940

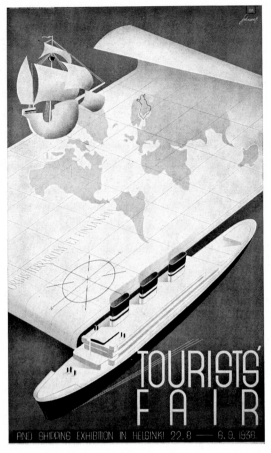

1   2

1. TOIVO WIKSTEDT: Poster designed by this gifted artist a short time before his death - Affiche dessinée par cet
éminent artiste peu de temps avant sa mort - Cartel dibujado por este eminente artista poco antes de su muerte

2. JORMA SUHONEN: Poster for the Tourist Fair and Shipping Exhibition in Helsinki 1938 - Affiche pour la
Foire du Tourisme et l'Exposition Maritime de Helsinki en 1938 - Cartel para la Feria del Turismo y Exposición Marí-
tima de Helsinki 1938

TOIVO WIKSTEDT: Poster - Affiche - Cartel

TOIVO WIKSTEDT: Poster - Affiche - Cartel

ONNI OJA: Book-cover - Couverture de livre Cubierta de libro

64

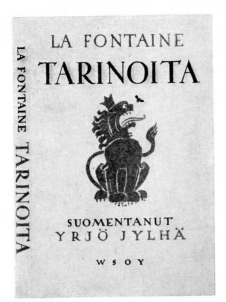

ONNI OJA: Book-covers - Couvertures de livres - Cubierta de libro

JORMA SUHONEN: Poster for the Finnish Air Traffic Company - Affiche pour la Société Finlandaise de Navigation aérienne - Cartel para "La Compañía Finlandesa de Tráfico Aéreo"

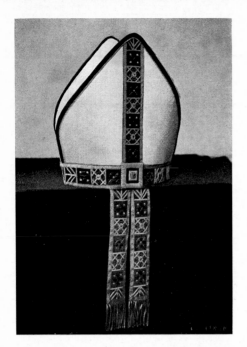

GRETA STRANDBERG: Bishop's mitre - Mitre - Mitra de Obispo
Suomen Käsityön Ystävät   Photo Pietinen

GRETA STRANDBERG: Bishop's chasuble. Suomen Käsityön Ystävät.
Handwoven fabric, designed by Laila Karttunen - Chasuble d'évêque,
exécutée par Suomen Käsityön Ystävät, tissée à la main. Dessin de Laila
Karttunen - Roquete de obispo, ejecutado por Suomen Käsityön Ystävät.
Tejido hecho a mano, dibujado por Laila Karttunen

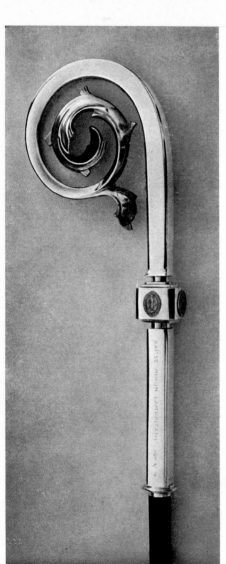

GUNNEL NYMAN: Bishop's crozier - Crosse d'évêque - Báculo de Obispo
O.Y. Taito A.B.

GUNILLA JUNG: Silver Altar Set for the Mikael Agricola Church in Helsinki,
executed by O.Y. Viri A.B. - Argenterie d'autel pour l'église Mikael Agricola
à Helsinki, exécutée par O.Y. Viri A.B. - Plata de Altar para la Iglesia Mikael
Agricola en Helsinki, ejecutado por O.Y. Viri A.B.

DORA JUNG: Damask
for Church use - Damas
pour usage ecclésiasti-
que - Damasco para uso
de Iglesia

In the metal-workshop - Dans l'atelier d'ouvrages en bronze et en laiton - Obras de bronce y de latón en el estudio

HENRY ERICSSON: Coffee Set in silver - Service à café en argent - Juego de café de plata, ejecutado por O.Y. Taito A.B.

68

HENRY ERICSSON: Chalice and Flagon in chased silver, designed for St. Paul's Church, Helsinki - Calice et gobelet en argent ciselé pour l'église St. Paul, Helsinki - Cáliz y cubilete de plata cincelada, para la Iglesia de San Pablo, Helsinki

GUNILLA JUNG: Coffee Set in silver, executed by Suomen Kultaseppäosakeyhtiö - Service à café en argent, exécuté par Suomen Kultaseppäosakeyhtiö - Juego de café de plata, ejecutado por Suomen Kultaseppäosakeyhtiö

Photo Iffland

GUNILLA JUNG: Silver cutlery - Coutellerie en argent - Cuchillos de plata
Kultakeskus, Hämeenlinna

RUNAR ENGBLOM: Pewter coffee set -
Service à café en étain - Juego de café en
estaño.   O.Y. Viri A.B.

GRETA SKOGSTER-LEHTINEN: Linen
damask for table cloth - Tissu damassé en
lin pour nappe - Damasco de lino para
mantel   Photo Rasmussen

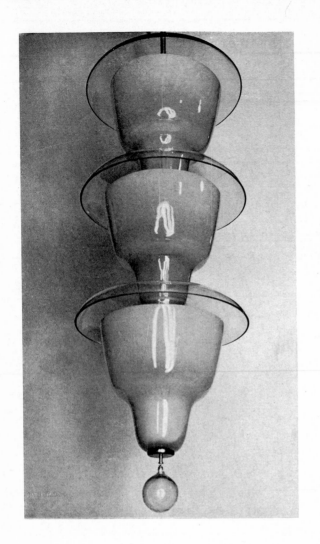

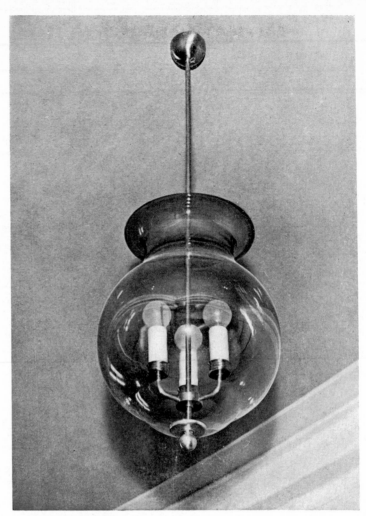

PAAVO TYNELL: Lighting fittings, executed by O.Y. Taito A.B. Glass from Riihimäki Glassworks - Lampes exécutées par O.Y. Taito A.B. Verres de la Verrerie de Riihimäki - Armazones de alumbrado, ejecutados por O.Y. Taito A.B. Cristal de la Fábrica de Cristal Riihimäki

Photo Kolmio

PAAVO TYNELL: Lighting fittings - Lampe - Armazón de alumbrado
O.Y. Taito A.B.   Photo Roos

GUNILLA JUNG: Lighting fittings - Lampe - Armazóm de alumbrado
O.Y. Orno A.B.   Photo Roos

GUNILLA JUNG: Table lamp - Lampe de table - Lámpara de mesa. O.Y. Orno A.B.
Photo Roos

TOINI MUONA: Vase and bowl in stoneware -
Vase et coupe en grès - Jarrón y copa de barro
O.Y. Arabia A.B.   Photo Kolmio

ELSA ELENIUS: Pottery - Céramique -
Cerámicas   Photo Kolmio

Potter's hands at the wheel
- Mains de potier au tour -
Manos de alfarero traba-
jando

TOINI MUONA: Jar in craquelée china - Cruche en porcelaine
craquelée - Jarro de porcelana con esmalte agrietado
O.Y. Arabia A.B.

TOINI MUONA: Pottery - Céramique - Cerámicas

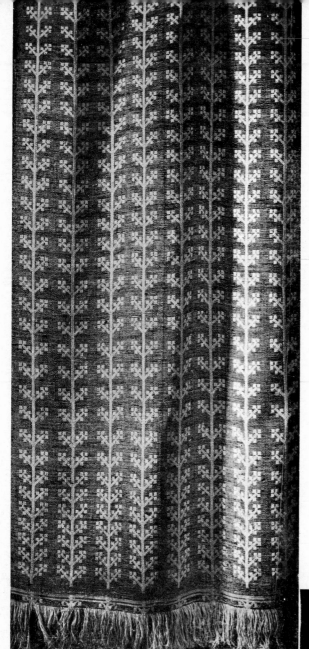

ARTTU BRUMMER: Glass Bottle. Riihimäki Glassworks - Coupe de verre. Verrerie de Riihimäki - Botella de cristal. Fábrica de cristal Riihimäki   Photo Kolmio

VIOLA GRÅSTEN: Linen furnishing fabric - Tissu en lin pour intérieur - Tejidos de lino para interiores

KURT EKHOLM: Pottery - Céramique - Cerámicas
          O.Y. Arabia A.B.

76

ELSA ELENIUS: Pottery - Céramique - Cerámicas

AUNE SIIMES: Fruit dish in stoneware-chamotte - Plat à fruits en chamotte - Plato de fruta en barro O.Y. Arabia A.B.
Photo Pietinen

SIIRI HARIOLA: Pottery - Céramique - Cerámicas
Photo Pietinen

DORA JUNG: Tablecloth in linen damask -
Nappe en tissu damassé en lin - Mantel en
damasco de lino

TOINI MUONA: Bowl with "sang de bœuf"
glaze - Coupe glacée sang de bœuf - Copa
vidriada "sang de bœuf"   O.Y. Arabia A.B.

Photo Saurén

MICHAEL SCHILKIN: Yak
in stoneware - Yack en grès
- Búfalo en barro
O.Y. Arabia A.B.

Photo Kolmio

78

MICHAEL SCHILKIN: Panther in stoneware - Panthère en grès - Pantera en
barro   Photo Saurén
O.Y. Arabia A.B.

SIIRI HARIOLA: Pottery - Céramique - Cerámicas

SIIRI HARIOLA: Pottery - Céramique - Cerámicas

PUBLISHED BY:
THE FINNISH SECTION OF NEW YORK WORLD'S FAIR 1939

EDITORS:
H. RÖNEHOLM W. WEST W. WAHLROOS

PRINTED BY;
SUOMALAISEN KIRJALLISUUDEN SEURAN KIRJAPAINON OY.
HELSINKI 1939